DK SUPER Economics

MONEY and TRADE

From ancient bartering to modern markets, explore the dynamic world of money and how we trade across the globe

PRODUCED FOR DK BY
Editorial Just Content Limited
Design Studio Noel

Author Allison Hay

Senior Editor Amelia Jones
Senior Art Editor Gilda Pacitti
Managing Editor Katherine Neep
Managing Art Editor Elizabeth Arnoux
Pre-Production Designer Rohit Singh
Production Controller Nancy-Jane Maun
Publisher Sarah Forbes
Managing Director, Learning Hilary Fine

First published in Great Britain in 2026 by
Dorling Kindersley Limited
20 Vauxhall Bridge Road,
London SW1V 2SA

The authorised representative in the EEA is
Dorling Kindersley Verlag GmbH. Arnulfstr. 124,
80636 Munich, Germany

Copyright © 2026 Dorling Kindersley Limited
A Penguin Random House Company
10 9 8 7 6 5 4 3 2 1
001–354564–Mar/2026

All rights reserved.
No part of this publication may be reproduced, stored in or introduced into a retrieval system, or transmitted, in any form, or by any means (electronic, mechanical, photocopying, recording, or otherwise), without the prior written permission of the copyright owner.
DK values and supports copyright. Thank you for respecting intellectual property laws by not reproducing, scanning or distributing any part of this publication by any means without permission. By purchasing an authorised edition, you are supporting writers and artists and enabling DK to continue to publish books that inform and inspire readers.
No part of this publication may be used or reproduced in any manner for the purpose of training artificial intelligence technologies or systems. In accordance with Article 4(3) of the DSM Directive 2019/790, DK expressly reserves this work from the text and data mining exception.

A CIP catalogue record for this book
is available from the British Library.
ISBN: 978-0-2417-7443-4

Printed and bound in China

www.dk.com

This book was made with Forest Stewardship Council™ certified paper – one small step in DK's commitment to a sustainable future.
Learn more at www.dk.com/uk/information/sustainability

Contents

What Is Money?	4
The History of Money	6
The History of Trade	8
Why Do We Need Money?	10
What Is a Market?	12
All About Banks	14
Different Ways to Pay	16
Touch It vs. Tap It	18
Borrowing Money	20
Overdrafts and Compound Interest	22
Money Risks	24
From There to Here: Imports	26
From Here to There: Exports	28
International Trade Agreements	30
The World Trade Organization	32
International Fairtrade	34
Trade Tariffs	36
Everyday Economics: From Pocket Money to Pay Cheques	38
Let's Try It! International Trade Game	40
Vocabulary Builder: All About Credit	42
Glossary	44
Index	46

Words in **bold** are explained in the glossary on page 44.

What Is MONEY?

"Money talks." "Time is money." "Money makes the world go around." These sayings remind us that money is more than just paper and coins. It powers our economy, decides how resources are shared and impacts **trade** worldwide. Knowing about money helps us understand how the world works.

Money is a **currency**. It can come in different amounts of paper money and coins, and varies from country to country. The British pound is the oldest currency in the world that is still in use today.

Every day, there are millions and millions of **transactions** involving money. This transaction at a flower market is just one example of money changing hands.

Think about it

How do you use money in your own life?

Money is a measure of **wealth**. The more money someone has, the wealthier they are. The wealthiest people in the world are billionaires. The first confirmed **billionaire** was the American oil **tycoon** John D. Rockefeller.

Money is a **medium**. From around 1821 to the 1930s, the **value** of money was tied to the value of gold. But today, this is no longer the case. Governments around the world decide how much money to print and **mint**.

Money makes it easy to trade goods and **services** worldwide. This cargo ship is an example of how countries transport **merchandise** to each other today.

We can use money to buy and sell goods in a marketplace. The marketplace might be a physical store or an online website. We can spend money with physical currency or use a **debit or credit card**.

The History of MONEY

People have used money to buy and sell things for thousands of years. It began in the 7th century BCE, when the Ancient Greeks started using metal coins as money. By the medieval period, societies from Europe to China were using metal coins to buy and sell. Coins made it easy to trade goods with other countries.

Coins held **intrinsic** value because they were made from metal, but paper banknotes were valued based on the silver and **gold standards**. Eventually, these standards were replaced by **exchange rates** in the 20th century.

In the 16th century, Spanish explorers arrived in the Americas looking for gold and silver. They found lots of it, which allowed more metal coins to be produced.

The first **banknotes** in Europe date back to 1661 and were issued by a bank in Sweden.

Paper money was used regularly by Chinese people from the 7th century because it was not as heavy as metal coins. This picture shows Chinese paper money from the 14th century.

Many coins today have a portrait of someone's face, such as a monarch or president. Alexander the Great (356–323 BCE) introduced this style during his reign as the king of Macedonia.

Some think money dates back further than we used to believe. The discovery of the Ishango bone, an artefact around 20,000 years old, suggests that people may have traded goods or services long ago. It has markings that seem to show counting or record-keeping.

Fascinating fact

The Cerro Rico mountain in Bolivia was the world's largest source of silver between the 16th and 18th century. This silver became the basis for an international silver currency.

The History of **TRADE**

Today, money is everywhere and is a big part of our lives. This means that it is easy to take it for granted. However, this was not always the case. Before human societies adopted currency as a means of buying and selling, they relied on other systems of **exchange**, such as **bartering**.

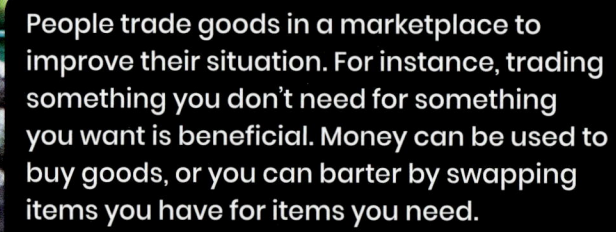

People trade goods in a marketplace to improve their situation. For instance, trading something you don't need for something you want is beneficial. Money can be used to buy goods, or you can barter by swapping items you have for items you need.

Before money was common, people often bartered. They traded goods like grain for shoes or tools. This system was used widely in medieval Europe, where coins weren't often available in rural areas.

In North America, Indigenous people and white settlers traded items like furs for blankets, cloth and tools. While Indigenous people used currencies like shells and beads, bartering remained common.

Swapping to save

People still barter today. For example, they might swap clothes. This can make trading easier, especially when people have extra goods they no longer need, or limited money.

Fascinating fact

The Silk Road is a famous ancient trade route. Traders sent goods such as spices and silk along this 6,400-km (4,000-mile) road for over 1,500 years.

Why Do We NEED MONEY?

Although bartering is one way to exchange goods, money makes it easier to trade because it has a set value. With bartering, people must agree on the value of each item. With money, they only need to agree on the price of the item being sold.

Food and drink are common items that people buy with money. The average UK household is estimated to spend about 16 per cent of its budget on these items each year.

People often use websites or social media to barter items like used electronics, including game consoles, laptops or smartphones.

Money also pays for services, which are acts people buy but can't physically store, unlike goods. Examples include health insurance and dentist visits.

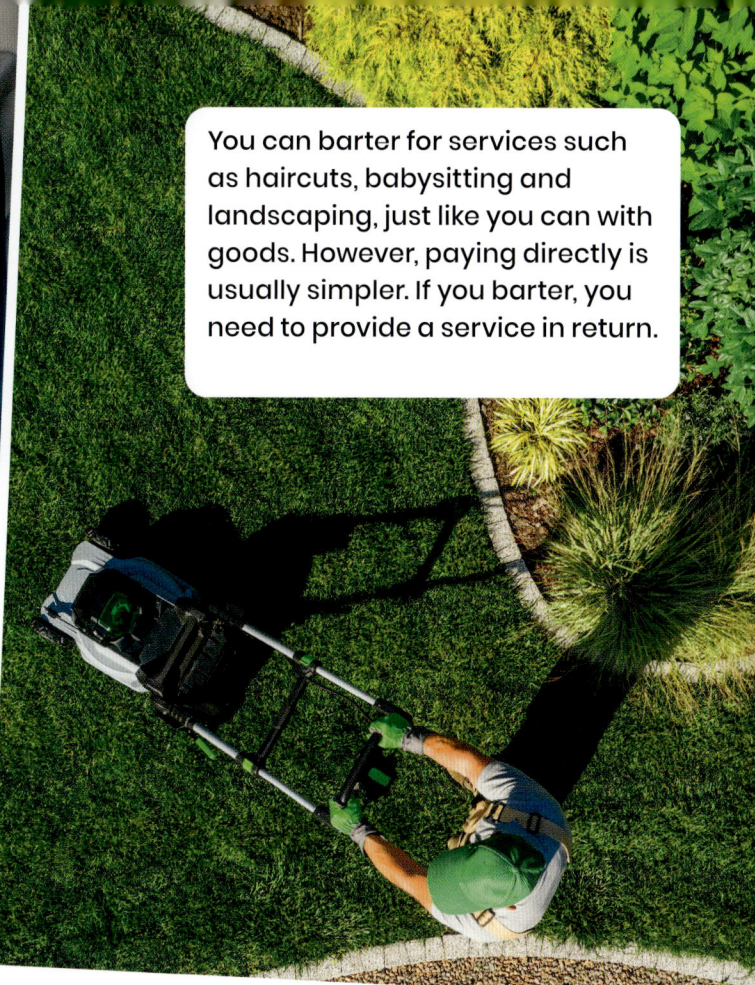

You can barter for services such as haircuts, babysitting and landscaping, just like you can with goods. However, paying directly is usually simpler. If you barter, you need to provide a service in return.

DIFFERENT DENOMINATIONS

Cash comes in a lot of different **denominations**. You can buy things with coins, paper money or a mix of the two.

Coins are useful when making smaller purchases. Standard denominations of coins include 1, 5, 10, 20 or 25 and 50. In the 20th century, you could still find unusual denominations of coins, like the British halfpenny. It was worth 1/480th of a pound.

Paper money is better for making larger purchases, so you do not have to count out lots of coins! Standard denominations of paper money include 1, 5, 10, 20 and 50. Some currencies, including the American dollar, come in 100s.

Fascinating fact

The Bank of England £100,000,000 note, also referred to as Titan, is a non-circulating banknote used to back the value of Scottish and Northern Irish banknotes. It is the highest denomination of banknote printed by the Bank of England.

What Is a MARKET?

In economics, a market is where buyers and sellers trade goods. It used to be a specific place where people gathered. Now, a market refers to a larger area, like a whole country, where goods and services are traded. Today, a market is more of a **concept** than a physical location. It is also central to **capitalism**, the primary economic system used around the world.

Capitalism originated from **mercantilism**, the central economic system in Europe and parts of Africa from the 16th to the 18th centuries. Under mercantilism, a country aimed to sell more goods to other countries and buy fewer goods from them. This helped to boost its wealth and power.

Under the reign of Queen Elizabeth I (1558 to 1603), England became a powerful centre of trade. Some of the goods England traded included furs, timber, dyes, dried fruit and cotton.

Capitalism started in the 18th century. In capitalism, the focus is more on the buyer and seller as individuals. The price of goods and services is determined by how much someone wants to buy them and whether there are lots of them or not.

Adam Smith was a Scottish economist in the 1700s who is credited with being the father of capitalism.

Think about it?

Adam Smith popularised the theory that the market is controlled by an invisible hand. This hand can't be seen but it works to fulfil the best interests of society. What do you think about this idea?

In command and capitalist economic systems, the market is an essential concept. But in capitalism, the market is a **free market**. This means that individual buyers and sellers determine the price of goods.

All About BANKS

If you have a lot of cash, you must store it somewhere. Most people keep their money in a bank, an institution where people can save their money safely. This has the advantage of keeping money safe from loss or **theft**.

Banks have been around for hundreds of years. Their origins can be traced back to ancient civilizations that used bank-like institutions as long ago as 2,000 BCE. Modern banks spread throughout Europe during the Renaissance, in the 15th and 16th centuries.

Think about it ??

How many banks do you have in your area?

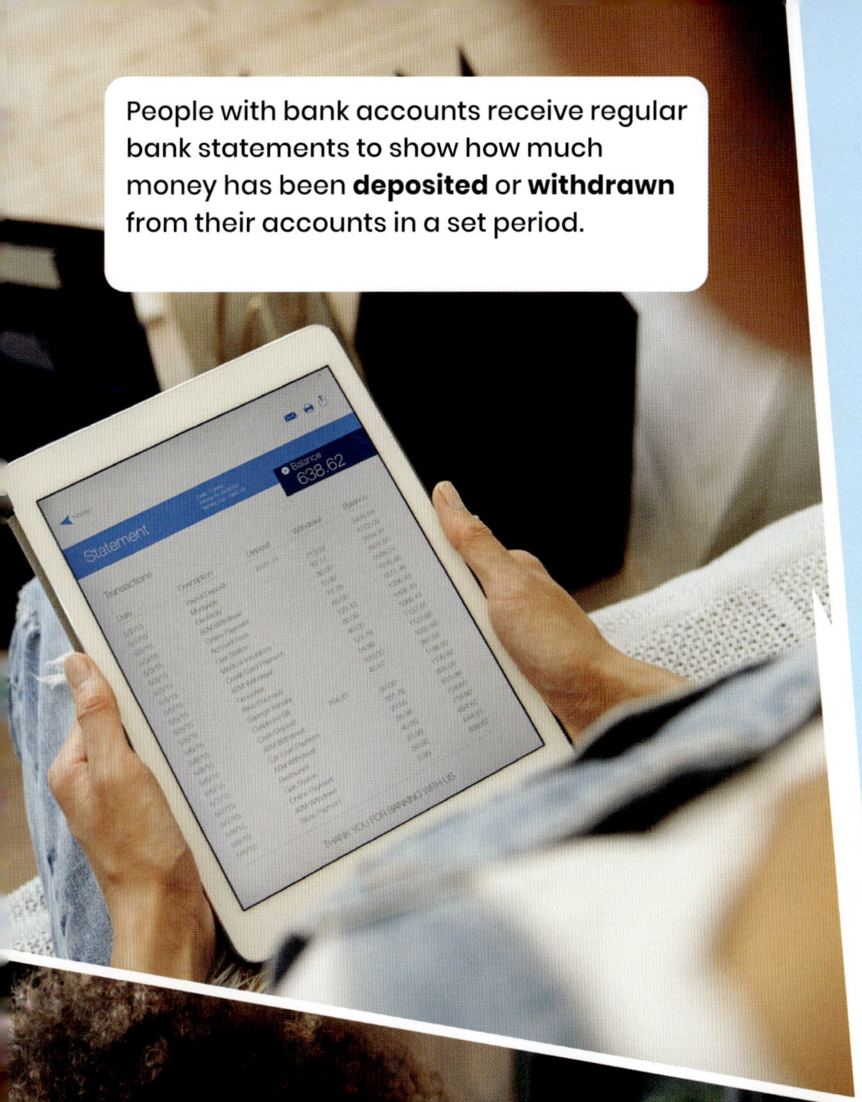

People with bank accounts receive regular bank statements to show how much money has been **deposited** or **withdrawn** from their accounts in a set period.

You can also use a bank to save your money. You can earn **interest** if you save your money in a savings account. This is another advantage of a bank account, whereas if you keep your money somewhere physical, like in your house, its value will stay the same.

Interest

Banks give you interest for keeping your money with them. They can use your money to lend to other customers, and in return you earn interest.

Say you have saved £100 in a savings account. The bank gives you an annual **interest rate** of 2 per cent.

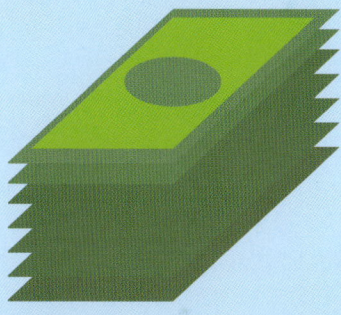

After one year, your £100 will become £102. This is because your initial £100 has earned 2-per cent interest, or £2. This is assuming you do not withdraw any of your savings before the end of the year.

COMPOUND INTEREST

Different Ways TO PAY

We use money to pay for things. Money comes in different forms, including coins, banknotes and debit cards. A debit card allows people to withdraw cash from an ATM (automated teller machine). People can also use a debit card to pay for goods and services directly, using contactless payment or **chip** and PIN (personal identification number).

You can use your card details on your phone to make a payment. This is called a cashless payment.

Fascinating fact

The first ATM opened in London in 1967.

An ATM allows you to withdraw money anytime without visiting a bank and speaking to a cashier.

People use debit cards to make purchases without cash. Contactless payments let users tap their card near a machine that checks for enough money in their account to make the payment. If contactless payment isn't an option, you might need to use your PIN. You insert your debit card, enter your PIN, and the machine checks with your bank to approve or deny the transaction.

People once used paper cheques for payments, but these are rare now. Unlike instant debit card transactions, stores would send cheques to their banks for processing. This delayed finding out if there were enough funds to make the payment.

No wallet? No problem!

A company in London has invented a special microchip that can be used to pay for goods and services. This microchip works just like the chip in a debit card, except it is inserted under people's skin! This man has a microchip under the skin at the base of his thumb.

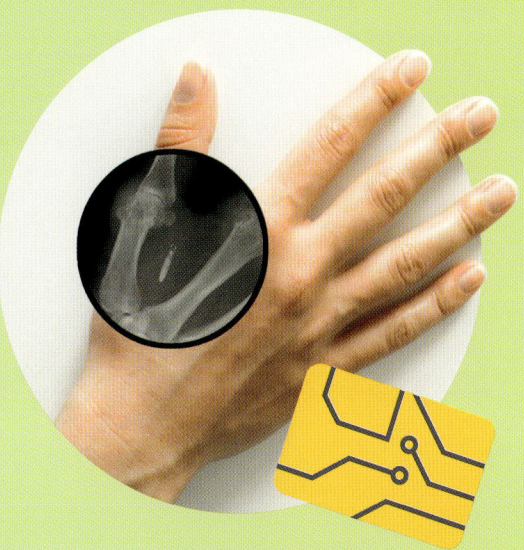

If you don't fancy having a microchip under your skin, you could choose **wearable tech** instead. People can pay with smart watches and rings. It means there is no need to reach for your wallet! These gadgets make it quick to pay, but easier to spend without thinking through the consequences.

Touch It vs. TAP IT

Just as there are many payment methods available today, there are also many places where we can pay for goods and services. Traditionally, people have paid for things in a marketplace. Nowadays, a marketplace can be physical or digital. This means we can go to a shop to buy goods or use a computer or smartphone to buy things online.

Paying in-person

ADVANTAGES
Paying in-person allows you to look at a product before you purchase it. You can usually take the item straight home and won't have to pay any shipping fees. You don't have to upload your card or bank data to the internet, so you don't have to worry about online fraud.

DISADVANTAGES
You have to travel to the shop, and you can only shop when the store is open. The store might be busy, and you could end up standing in a long line, waiting to be served. If you pay in-person and then lose the receipt, you won't be able to return the item or get your money back.

Paying online

ADVANTAGES
When you shop online, you can browse and pay anytime, and anywhere. It is usually easy to read reviews and find the best deals by looking on different sites. The items you buy are shipped to your home, so you don't have to carry heavy bags or travel to a shopping centre.

DISADVANTAGES
You don't get your item straight away, and when it arrives, it might not look or work how you thought it would. When you pay online, you have to enter your bank details and personal information, so you are at risk if the websites you visit are not secure.

Fascinating fact

One of the first online transactions took place in 1994. A man named Dan Kohn sold a CD to a friend on a website he had created called NetMarket.

Borrowing MONEY

People use cash and debit cards to pay for goods and services with the money they have in their bank accounts. But what if you need to pay for something and you do not have the funds to cover the transaction? In this case, you can sometimes borrow money from your bank through a credit card or a **loan**.

A credit card is like a debit card but does not use money from your bank account. Instead, you have a credit limit, which is the most you can spend.

With savings accounts, the money in the account earns interest over a year that you get to keep. But with a credit card, the money you have spent earns interest over the year you must pay back. The interest rate is usually quite high – sometimes over 30 per cent.

Why people use loans

Besides credit cards, people use loans to borrow money. When you get a loan, a bank lends you a specific amount of money you must repay over time, along with interest. If you borrow £1,000, you will repay more than £1,000.

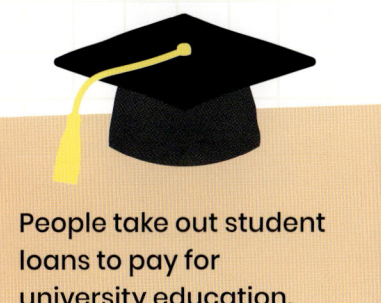

People take out student loans to pay for university education.

People take out loans to pay for new cars.

People take out loans, or **mortgages**, to pay for new apartments or houses.

People take out personal loans to pay for all sorts of things, like home improvements, holidays or medical expenses.

People take out business loans to start a new business or to pay for business **expenses**.

People take out loans to pay for emergencies they have not planned for.

Fascinating fact

Mesopotamians, from a region in southwestern Asia, gave loans to each other as far back as 3,000 BCE. They loaned goods such as grain and livestock. They left records of this on stone tablets.

Overdrafts and COMPOUND INTEREST

A loan can be a very useful tool for people who need to pay for goods and services they would not otherwise be able to **afford**. But loans, including **overdrafts**, can also cause problems. People can end up **owing** a lot more money than they borrowed.

Fascinating fact

The Ancient Romans allowed lenders to charge simple interest on loans. But they made compound interest illegal, believing it was unreasonable and would harm society.

An overdraft is a common way in which people with bank accounts can borrow money. With an overdraft, you can pay for goods and services even when your bank account is empty. Banks often charge a high interest rate on overdrafts, so people often owe even more money.

The cost of borrowing

1

YEAR ONE:
£200,000
BORROWED WITH 5% INTEREST

Say you have bought a house. The bank lends you £200,000. This is your mortgage. The bank charges an annual interest rate of 5 per cent.

2

YEAR TWO:
£210,000
OWED AFTER YEAR ONE

The £200,000 you borrowed will become £210,000 after one year. This is because your initial £200,000 has been charged 5 per cent interest, or £10,000.

3

YEAR TWENTY:
£530,660
OWED AFTER 20 YEARS

After 20 years, your £200,000 will become more than £530,660. That is more than double the amount you borrowed. This is because the mortgage amount has been charged 5 per cent interest each year. The interest has been added to the amount you first borrowed.

Lenders usually use compound interest, which means they charge interest on the original amount you borrowed, as well as on any added interest from before. This is common for overdrafts, mortgages and student loans, and can greatly increase the amount you owe over time.

You need to make regular payments on a mortgage to reduce the debt. Otherwise, the amount you owe can grow very large due to compound interest.

Money RISKS

Banks can be great places to store and save money, mainly because they help you earn interest on your cash. They are a more secure place to keep your money than storing it in a cookie jar. But while you might think money in a bank account is always safe, there are still risks.

Some people, especially children, store their money in a money bank at home. This is a good option if you only store small amounts of money. This way, it is not a big deal if you lose the jar or someone steals it.

When you carry cash or store it at home, there is always a possibility that it might be stolen. This is one of the risks of keeping cash. But money stored in a bank account can also be stolen by **phishers**, **scammers** and other committers of online **fraud**.

Think about it

British people lost more than £17 billion to scams and fraud in 2023. What do you think people can do to keep their money safe?

ONLINE THREATS

Phishing is a method in which a scammer (or phisher) tries to trick someone into giving them their personal information, bank information or even money.

Scamming includes phishing, but it also includes other methods for deceiving people out of their money, such as **identity theft**, **extortion** and **blackmail**.

Fraud is the legal term for trying to deceive other people in order to benefit oneself. Phishing and scamming are examples of fraud.

Phishing and fraud happen when personal information isn't secure. Protecting your details is vital, and banks must also ensure they keep your information safe.

From There to Here: IMPORTS

In our globalised society, it is important for different countries to trade with each other. This benefits both countries, as trade allows them to get things they do not have and give things they have lots of. When a government pays for a good or service that is produced abroad, it is called an **import**.

People have been trading with each other for thousands and thousands of years. For example, there is research on trading dating back around 300,000 years where weapons made from obsidian were found in Southern Kenya. As obsidian was not available in this area, this find suggested it was traded from a different country.

Fascinating fact

It is estimated that 90 per cent of the world's goods are transported by sea.

Many countries import food from other countries. The UK imports many fresh fruits and vegetables from South Africa, including apples, pears, avocados and grapes.

In the UK, most clothing is imported. The primary clothing market in the world is China. In 2024, China produced 32 per cent of the world's clothing!

As Europe's largest economy, Germany imports a lot of raw materials, electronics and pharmaceuticals, mainly from China, the Netherlands and France.

Importing services

Countries offer services to one another in a process called **outsourcing**. This means that businesses in one country pay businesses in another to do work for them. For example, customer service call centres are often outsourced.

Data centres are very large buildings filled with computers that deliver the internet services we use. The US has the most data centres in the world, with nearly 3,000. Lots of countries outside of the US use these services.

From Here to There: EXPORTS

When a country sells a good or service that it produces **domestically** to a country abroad, this is called an **export**. Just like imports, exports are an essential way countries trade with each other and generate income.

The Japanese Empire (1868–1947) was a major silk exporter to the rest of the world. In fact, it controlled 80 per cent of the world's silk production.

Think about it

How many products do you have that has a "Made in…" label?

As with imports, the US also exports services to other countries. One of the US's major exports is cars. Canada is the biggest market for US-made cars. The country imported around $35.6 billion worth of American cars in 2024.

The US exports a lot of food. It is also the world's major exporter of tree nuts to other countries. A total of 10 per cent of all the exported tree nuts in the world come from the US.

World leaders

Brazil leads the world in coffee production and is a key exporter. People around the world enjoy Brazilian coffee for its strong and rich taste.

Switzerland is famous for making high-quality watches. Well-known brands such as Rolex, Patek Philippe and TAG Heuer are popular worldwide and make up much of Switzerland's sales to other countries.

International Trade AGREEMENTS

Imports and exports form the basis of international trade between different countries. They have also led to the creation of international trade agreements. These are rules around buying and selling goods and services that countries agree to follow.

Many countries engaged in **protectionism** before international trade agreements became widespread. This term refers to any method a country might use to restrict imports from other countries. Protectionism aims to increase a country's production of goods and services, but it often hurts the economy.

The Bretton Woods conference in 1944 was a major global meeting between the US, UK and 42 other countries. It led to the creation of the World Bank and the International Monetary Fund to help achieve economic stability and peace after World War II.

The conference was held at the famous Mount Washington Hotel in Jefferson, New Hampshire, from 1 to 22 July 1944. 730 Delegates attended the conference.

The General Agreement on Tariffs and Trade (GATT) was finalised in 1947. In contrast with protectionist policies, the purpose of the GATT was to increase international trade and remove trade barriers. In this way, it supported **free trade**. It was replaced in 1995 by the creation of the **World Trade Organization**.

The first ever GATT meeting was held in Geneva, Switzerland.

Fascinating fact

The Cobden-Chevalier Treaty of 1860 was the first international free trade agreement. It was between France and the UK and made trading goods between the countries cheaper and easier.

The European Union is one well-known example of an international trade agreement between multiple countries. The 27 European Union countries and 3 European Economic Area countries have a single trade policy. This makes trade between the countries very easy.

The World Trade ORGANIZATION

The World Trade Organization (WTO) was founded in January 1995. It counts 166 member countries, making up 98 per cent of all world trade. The WTO is the only international organisation dealing with trade between nations. The trade agreements that come out of the WTO are signed by all the members and **ratified**.

Dr Ngozi Okonjo-Iweala has been the Director-General of the WTO since 2021. She is the first woman and the first African person to hold this position.

The WTO headquarters is located in Geneva, Switzerland.

PROTECTING IDEAS IN GLOBAL TRADE

The WTO oversees four international trade agreements: GATT, the General Agreement on Trade in Services (GATS), an agreement on **intellectual property** rights (TRIPS) and an agreement on investment (TRIMS). Intellectual property includes things such as patents, copyrights and trademarks.

Jonathan Kelly invented Squishmallows in 2017. Squishmallows became a registered trademark on 24 April 2018, which provides the company with tools to prevent their design from being used.

Fascinating fact

Dr Okonjo-Iweala is a distinguished economist. She has college degrees from Harvard and Massachusetts Institute of Technology (MIT), and over 20 honorary degrees from universities around the world.

Globalisation refers to economic and cultural **interdependence** among different countries. The WTO plays a key role in our globalised world, helping world economies run more smoothly. It is a place for member countries to discuss trade issues, especially if there are disagreements. It also allows countries to come to agreements on trade policy.

International FAIRTRADE

Fairtrade is an international movement that seeks to improve trade relationships for people who produce goods in **developing countries**. Many products, such as bananas, coffee, and chocolate, are certified as Fairtrade and have a Fairtrade label. The movement was founded in 1992 with the help of numerous charities, including Oxfam, Christian Aid and the World Development Movement.

Small farms in the developing world often produce coffee beans. Fairtrade farmers are paid fair prices for their crops, which helps them to support their families and develop their communities. The Fairtrade label on coffee shows that farmers received fair treatment.

There are more Fairtrade producers of coffee than any other product.

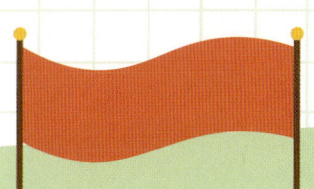

Today's Fairtrade movement can be traced back to the "Trade not Aid" slogan of the 1960s. It was adopted by the United Nations and emphasised improving trade in developing countries.

Cocoa takes up the most land of any Fairtrade product globally. In 2022, over 1.5 million hectares of land were devoted to growing cocoa beans.

The first Fairtrade food products were tea and coffee, followed by dried fruit and cocoa.

The US is the third largest market for Fairtrade goods. In 2023, sales of Fairtrade products were over $1.2 billion.

Fairtrade works with more than 1,900 producers in 68 countries around the world.

Non-food items such as clothing, jewellery and homewares can also be certified as Fairtrade.

Flowers are the biggest Fairtrade product in the world. In 2022, over 950 million Fairtrade flowers were sold.

Fascinating fact

Fairtrade towns make up the base of a movement that started in the UK and spread to other countries. A Fairtrade town is a community that supports fair trade products by regularly purchasing them.

Trade TARIFFS

An important goal of international trade agreements is to reduce trade barriers. These can include **tariffs** and **customs duties**. A tariff is a tax on imports or exports. When a country puts a tariff on imports, it often does so to boost its economy. However, tariffs can backfire. They can cause the other country to put tariffs on exports, leading to higher prices for everyone.

Alexander Hamilton introduced three tariffs while serving as Secretary of the Treasury (1789–1795).

Tariffs were common in the US from the Revolutionary War period (1775) until the Civil War (1865). They were primarily used to raise money for the government.

The Tariff Act of 1930 put tariffs on more than 20,000 imports to the US. It caused many other countries to put tariffs on their exports to the US. Today, historians believe that this act made the economic hardship known as the **Great Depression** worse.

The North American Free Trade Agreement (NAFTA) was introduced in 1993 when Bill Clinton was president. It lasted until 2020. It was a trade agreement between the US, Mexico, and Canada. It immediately ended most tariffs between Mexico and the US.

Fascinating fact

In 1933, average tariff rates were almost 20 per cent. In 2019, this number was less than 2 per cent.

In more modern times, the US has placed tariffs on goods such as solar panels, lithium batteries for electric vehicles and steel. But the items with the highest tariffs are actually knitted or crocheted clothing!

Everyday ECONOMICS
From Pocket Money to Pay Cheque

Learning about money and trade helps us understand how local and global economies work. It can help in understanding why individual people and countries make the choices they do. Studying economics makes real-world issues relevant and relatable. It can also equip you with the skills you need to move throughout the world.

Bartering is an everyday activity among children. For example, you may know someone who trades Pokémon cards. Usually, one card is exchanged for another. Or a card might be traded for a different toy or other good.

You may already be familiar with money as you may receive regular **pocket money** or otherwise receive cash you then go on to spend. Understanding what money is, how it makes trading goods and services easier and what some of its risks are can better help you as you use money throughout your life.

As you get older, you will likely have a bank account and may need to borrow money. Understanding interest rates, compound interest and how loans work will better equip you to make sound financial decisions.

Learning about how globalisation affects the world can give you a greater insight into how global economies work. International trade agreements, imports, exports and tariffs can help us understand current events and inequalities between countries.

What can you do?

During your next shopping trip with an adult, look for the Fairtrade symbol on products such as chocolate, bananas and tea. Choose one of the products and make a poster or drawing to show where it comes from and why fair trade is important.

Let's TRY IT!

INTERNATIONAL TRADE GAME

Play a card game to help you understand how tariffs affect international trade. You are a country aiming to make as much money on imports and exports as possible. Will you have the strongest economy, or will another player impose a tariff on your goods?

You will need:
- A deck of cards, including jokers
- One to three other people to play with

AIM OF THE GAME:
Make as many packs of four matching cards of different suits as possible. The more books you make, the more money your country has.

1
Shuffle the cards. Deal seven cards to each player. The rest of the cards should be placed face-down in a draw pile.

2
The youngest player goes first. This player asks another player for a specific card. You want to make a book of four matching cards of different suits (such as four jacks).

3
If a player has the card you ask for, they must give it to you. If they do not have it, they say, "Go fish", and you draw a card from the draw pile.

4
Playing the joker: If a player asks you for a card that you do have, you can play the joker instead, if you have it in your set. This means the player asking you for the card will miss their turn. You also have to discard a second card from your deck, so it can also make it harder for you to win!

5
Gameplay continues clockwise until one player runs out of cards. When this happens, you must count who has the most books. The player with the most books wins. Congratulations! This player has the strongest economy.

Thailand exports rice to countries such as China and South Africa. Some importing countries may apply tariffs on foreign rice to protect their own farmers.

Vocabulary BUILDER
All About Credit

How can we make good financial choices, especially when it comes to borrowing money? Read this fictional blog entry by a finance blogger to learn more about credit.

BY MADDIE SANCHEZ

Hi all! Welcome to another issue of my finance blog. Today, we're going to look at credit. What is it, why is it important and what does it really mean to us?

Credit is your ability to borrow money and can be measured by something called a credit score. The higher it is, the better your credit and the more likely a bank will lend to you. If it's on the lower side, you might struggle to get a loan.

People can get bad credit scores when they don't pay back their loans, miss payments or have lots of credit cards. Once you get a low credit score, it can take a long time and a lot of work to build it back up.

I hope this has helped explain some of the basics of credit. It can have a huge impact on your life, so understanding it at a basic level can be a great way to help you make good financial choices.

Until next time!

Money nouns account, cash, credit, credit score, debt, goods, interest, interest rate, lender, loan, services, wealth

Money verbs apply, approve, borrow, buy, deny, increase, lend, pay back, repay, save, spend, take out

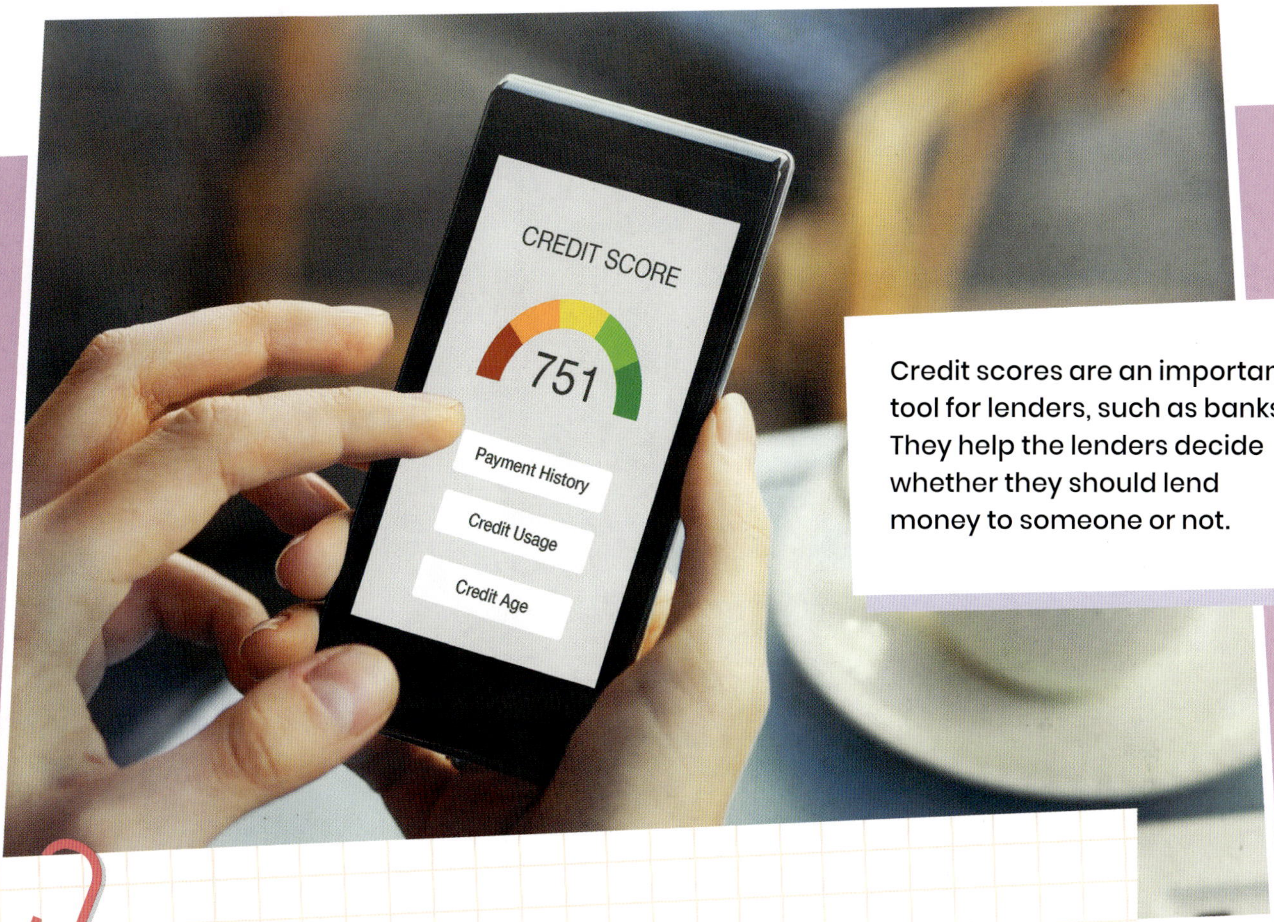

Credit scores are an important tool for lenders, such as banks. They help the lenders decide whether they should lend money to someone or not.

Imagine you work for a bank, and you are writing a blog about lending money. Use the words in the vocabulary box above, and the example on page 42 to help you.

- How would you explain what a loan is?
- How would you decide who to lend money to?
- What advice would you give to people who need to borrow money?

Glossary

Afford To have enough money to pay for something.

Allowance A set amount of money given regularly as payment for doing chores.

Banknote A piece of paper money, also called a bill.

Bartering Trading one good for another.

Billionaire Someone who is worth at least one billion of a currency, for example one billion pounds.

Blackmail Threatening someone to pay money so a secret is not revealed about them.

Capitalism The economic system in which organisations own and control resources and production facilities, such as factories, and try to earn profits.

Chip A very small piece of material that can store information.

Concept A thought or idea.

Credit card A card that lets you borrow money to pay for goods and services.

Currency The money used in a particular country.

Debit card A card that lets you use the money in your bank account to pay for goods and services.

Denomination The type or value of something.

Deposited Put into a bank account.

Domestically Relating to the country where one lives.

Exchange Another term for trade.

Exchange rate How much one currency can be traded for another; for example, the exchange rate of £1 might be $1.32.

Expense An amount of money spent on a good or service.

Export A good or service sent to one country from another country.

Extortion A crime in which someone forces someone else to give them money.

Fraud A crime in which someone tricks someone into giving them something, especially money.

Free market A fundamental principle in capitalism, where the economy is based on supply and demand with little governmental oversight.

Free trade The exchange of goods and services between countries without taxes, tariffs or other restrictions.

Globalisation The interconnectedness and interdependence of the world's economies and people.

Gold standard A system where the value of a currency is tied to an amount of gold.

Great Depression A severe worldwide economic downturn that lasted from 1929 until the late 1930s.

Hacker Someone who illegally breaks into websites, computer systems or networks.

Identity theft A crime in which someone steals another person's information to commit fraud or other crimes.

Import A product brought in from another country to be sold.

Intellectual property A good that someone creates using their creativity, such as a book or a design.

Interdependence Two or more things that are dependent on each other.

Interest The extra money you earn or pay when you borrow or save money.

Interest rate The cost of borrowing money, shown as a percentage.

Intrinsic The inherent quality of something.

Loan An amount of money you borrow from someone else and have to pay back.

Medium A means or way of doing something else.

Mercantilism The economic system in which a country exports lots of goods to other countries in order to increase its wealth and world power.

Merchandise Another term for goods that can be bought and sold.

Mint To produce coins.

Mortgage A loan you take out to pay for an apartment or house.

Outsourcing When a company pays another company to do work for them. Often, this work is done in a different country, where it costs less.

Overdraft A loan from the bank that covers you if you spend more money than you have in your account. It often comes with fees.

Owing Having to pay back.

Phisher A scammer who tries to trick other people into giving up personal information or payment details.

Protectionism Government policies that put up barriers to international trade, for example by increasing tariffs.

Ratified Approved or signed into law.

Scammer Someone who tries to trick people out of their money or possessions.

Service Something that another person provides and has value.

Tariff A tax on goods and services imported into a country.

Trade The exchange of goods between people, groups or countries.

Transaction An exchange or transfer of goods or services.

Tycoon A powerful, influential and wealthy businessperson.

Value How much something is worth, either in terms of money or more generally.

Wealth The value of all the things, including money, that someone owns.

Withdrawn Taken out of a bank account.

World Trade Organisation An international organisation that sets trade rules between different countries and works to improve economic development of all countries.

Index

A
agreements, international trade 30–31
Alexander the Great 7
allowance 38
Ancient Romans 22
ATMs (automated teller machines) 16–17

B
banknotes 6–7, 11
banks 14–15
    risks 24–25
bartering 8, 9, 10, 11
Bolivia 7
borrowing money 20–23
Brazil 29
Bretton Woods conference 30
British pound 4

C
Canada 29, 37
capitalism 12–13
cashless payments 16
cheques, paper 17
China 7, 27
chip and PIN 16
Clinton, Bill 37
Cobden-Chevalier Treaty 31
cocoa 35

coffee 29, 34, 35
coins 6–7, 11
compound interest 22–23
contactless payments 17
credit cards 20
currencies 4, 9
customs duties 36

D
data centres 27
debit cards 16, 17
denominations 11

E
economics 38–39
Elizabeth I, Queen 12
England 12
    see also UK
European Union 31
exchange 8
exports 28–29

F
Fairtrade 34–35
flowers 35
food and drink 10, 29
France 27, 31
fraud 25
free market 13

G
game, international trade 40–41
General Agreement on Tariffs and Trade (GATT) 31, 33
General Agreement on Trade in Services (GATS) 33
Germany 27
globalisation 33, 39
gold 6
Great Depression 37

H
Hamilton, Alexander 36
history
    of money 6–7
    of trade 8–9

I
imports 26–27, 37
in-person, paying 18
Indigenous people 9
intellectual property rights 33
interest 15, 20–21
    compound 22–23
International Monetary Fund 30
international trade agreements 30–33

investment, agreement on 33
Ishango bone 7

J
Japanese Empire 28

K
Kelly, Jonathan 33

L
loans 20, 21
    and compound interest 22–23

M
market 12–13
marketplace 5, 8, 18
mercantilism 12
Mesopotamia 21
Mexico 37
microchips 17
mortgages 21, 23
Mount Washington Hotel (Jefferson) 30

N
Netherlands, The 27
North American Free Trade Agreement (NAFTA) 37

O
Okonjo-Iweala, Ngozi 32, 33
online
    fraud 25
    paying 19
outsourcing 27
overdrafts 22

P
paper money 6–7, 11
paying for things 16–19
personal information 25
phishing 25
protectionism 30

R
rice 41
risks 24–25
Rockefeller, John D. 5

S
savings
    bank accounts 15, 20
scamming 25
services 11
Silk Road 9
silver 6, 7
Smith, Adam 12
South Africa 27
Squishmallows 33
swapping 9
Sweden 7
Switzerland 29, 31, 32

T
tariffs 36–37
Thailand 41
transactions 4
tree nuts 29
TRIMS/TRIPS 33

U
UK (United Kingdom) 17, 27, 30, 31, 35
United States
    Bretton Woods conference 30
    Fairtrade 35
    imports 27
    international trade agreements 29
    tariffs 36–37

V
value of money 5, 6

W
wealth 5
wearable tech 17
World Bank 30
World Trade Organization (WTO) 31, 32–33

Acknowledgments

The publisher would like to thank the following for their kind permission to reproduce their photographs:

(Key: a-above; b-below/bottom; c-centre; f-far; l-left; r-right; t-top)

4 Getty Images: gerenme (cr). **Shutterstock.com:** Artem Varnitsin (b). **5 Alamy Stock Photo:** Pictorial Press Ltd (tl). **Getty Images:** Xavier Lorenzo (br); ponsulak (tr). **Shutterstock.com:** Studio concept (bl). **6 Alamy Stock Photo:** Granger Historical Picture Archive (bl); World History Archive (c). **Bridgeman Images:** Don Troiani. All Rights Reserved 2025 (clb, bc). **7 Alamy Stock Photo:** 2d Alan King (cr); Nigel Reed QEDimages (tl); Peter Horree (cra). **Bridgeman Images:** (tr); Universal History Archive / UIG (tr/overlay). Royal Belgian Institute of Natural Sciences: (bl). **8 Dreamstime.com:** Aleksandar Todorovic (bl). **8-9 Alamy Stock Photo:** The Granger Collection (b). **Bridgeman Images:** Tarker (t). **9 Getty Images:** Antagain (cr); everydayplus (crb). **Shutterstock.com:** oneinchpunch (cra). **10 Getty Images:** andresr (t); SeventyFour (b). **11 Dreamstime.com:** Eric Krouse (bl). Getty Images: demaerre (tl); mkos83 (br). **Shutterstock.com:** Virrage Images (tr). **12-13 Getty Images:** Neme Jimenez (background). **12 Alamy Stock Photo:** IanDagnall Computing (bc). **Bridgeman Images:** Mondadori Portfolio / Electa (cl). **13 Alamy Stock Photo:** Science History Images (tr); The Granger Collection (cl). **Getty Images:** georgeclerk (bl). **14 Alamy Stock Photo:** Nikreates. **15 Getty Images:** monkeybusinessimages (tl); VioletaStoimenova (bl). **16 Shutterstock.com:** Gorodenkoff (bl). **17 Alamy Stock Photo:** Oleg Breslavtsev (cr). **Getty Images:** Jana Murr (cl); zamrznutitonovi (t); sampsyseeds (bl); Andrei Nasonov (br). **18 Alamy Stock Photo:** Enrique Shore (bl). Shutterstock.com: voronaman (c). **19 Getty Images:** andresr (t); brizmaker (c); Octavian Lazar (b). **20 Alamy Stock Photo:** Dmitrii Melnikov. **22 Getty Images:** blackCAT. **23 Shutterstock.com:** G-Stock Studio. **24 Getty Images:** fcafotodigital. **25 Shutterstock.com:** fizkes. **26 Alamy Stock Photo:** North Wind Picture Archives (bl). **27 Getty Images:** AscentXmedia (tl); Wengen Ling (cl); sturti (cr); SweetBunFactory (bl). Shutterstock.com: IM Imagery (br). **28 Bridgeman Images:** Stefano Bianchetti (cl/overlay). **Getty Images:** zhuzhu (bl). **28-29 Dreamstime.com:** Barmalini (bc). **Getty Images:** 6381380 (tc). **29 Getty Images:** Robert Kirk (br). **Shutterstock.com:** Tetiana Tychynska (tr). **30 Alamy Stock Photo:** Joerg Hackemann (br); World History Archive (bl); SocialHistoryImages (cr). **31 Alamy Stock Photo:** Andia (b); Photo 12 (tr/overlay). Getty Images: pawel.gaul (t). **32 Alamy Stock Photo:** olrat (b). **Getty Images:** Joel Saget (cr). **33 Alamy Stock Photo:** Katie Collins, Stockimo (t); dpa picture alliance (b). **34 Alamy Stock Photo:** Simon Rawles (b). **Getty Images:** wundervisuals (cl/overlay). **36 Alamy Stock Photo:** GL Archive (t); World History Archive (b). **37 Alamy Stock Photo:** Ronnie Chua (c); IanDagnall Computing (t); Rob Crandall (cr/overlay); Free Belarus! (bl). **38 Getty Images:** MesquitaFMS (clb). **Shutterstock.com:** Kittyfly (cr). **39 Alamy Stock Photo:** Digital Image Library (t). **Getty Images:** Thinglass (b). **40 Shutterstock.com:** Gilmanshin. **41 Getty Images:** enviromantic (br). **42 Dreamstime.com:** Elswarro (cr). **43 Getty Images:** anyaberkut.

Cover images: *Front:* **Dorling Kindersley:** Dreamstime.com t; **Getty Images / iStock:** wundervisuals br; **Shutterstock.com:** Sven Hansche cr, i_am_zews bl; *Back:* **Alamy Stock Photo:** The Granger Collection tl; **Getty Images:** ponsulak cl, SweetBunFactory bl.